# VIKING
## JV RECRUITING

Enlist Today

# Chapter 1:

# Intro to JVs & Affiliates

## What are JVs?

Traditionally, JVs or Joint Venture Partners, simply referred to people who came together to cooperate and share in a business venture. Today, especially in the Internet Marketing (IM) world, it means something a little different. "JV" has become shorthand for "affiliate", or someone who sends traffic to your offer and is paid a commission for each sale they make. Frankly, this has caused a little confusion because, even in IM, you can still have a JV partnership in the traditional sense. For example, if you have a video course and ebook you created, but no skills or means for getting it online, you could partner with someone who will do the web design and development and split profits 50/50. The fact that those two JV partners will usually start recruiting "affiliates" to drive traffic to their product while calling those affiliates "JVs" makes things even more confusing, especially when you consider that those two JV partners split profits AFTER payouts are first made to "their JVs" (affiliates). This happens all the time in IM and so it's difficult to know what a person means when they say "would you like to be my JV?". But today, for whatever reason, 9 times out of 10 a person simply means affiliate. Frankly, conflating the terms was a horrible mistake on the part of the IM community.

That said, since it has become the norm, in this guide we'll be using the term "JV" to refer to affiliates. Clear as mud? Good. Let's move on...

## Why JVs Are Better (Than Paid Ads)

There are plenty of ways to drive traffic today. But generally, when you need to drive large amounts of it for a product launch, you'll be using paid methods. In many industries, the standard is, of course, paid advertising - usually pay-per-click or PPC. This is risky because you are paying out money for traffic without a guarantee that those clicks you paid for will convert to sales. So you're risking loss and you have little or no control of what your ROI will be. For example, you might pay $200 for 200 clicks and only make $210 from the handful of sales you made. It's great that you at least broke even, but you had no control over that outcome and in the next campaign you might make back less than you spent. You can still make this model work, obviously, but it requires a lot of testing, tweaking, adjusting, and a ton of "ad spend" just to get to the point where you've optimized and gained better control over your expected ROI.

Compare that to the JV/affiliate model. When you do a JV-driven product launch, you don't have to worry about ad spend. You're only paying for successful sales after they happen and you know in advance what amount you're paying per sale. You also don't have to spend any time or money testing and tweaking and targeting. You're handing all that hard work over to JVs with their own lists and audiences that they already know well and know how to pitch and market to.

When you compare the two, clearly the JV/affiliate model holds an advantage, especially if you're an independent entrepreneur and not a business with a huge advertising budget. Bottom line: if you want to launch a digital product, you need JVs sending traffic to your offer or you can kiss your dreams of having a big buyers list goodbye. The question is, how do you attract these JVs. It all starts with having an awesome JV recruiting page and that's what we'll cover next.

# Chapter 2:

# The Perfect JV Page

Before you start generating buzz about your launch among JVs, you need somewhere to send them. Theoretically, at an absolute minimum, you could send them to the JV registration page for the marketplace or affiliate platform you are using (e.g. your JVZoo or WarriorPlus affiliate details page). However, this would be unlikely to encourage sign-ups. Instead, what you need to do is show/tell them **why** they should promote your product as well as provide them with tools and resources to help them promote your product as easily as possible. The way you do this is by creating a JV page.

A JV page should ideally have the following components:

- An invite video describing your launch
- A visualization of your sales funnel
- A breakdown of your commission model
- A list of contest prizes
- A contest leader board
- An opt-in form for your JV email list
- A collection of DFY bonuses
- A bonus page template
- A supply of email swipes
- A collection of banners/graphics
- A JV blog
- A link to a sales page preview
- A prominent affiliate sign-up button

Let's look at each of these more closely.

## JV Invite Video

Your JV invite video is most effective if it features you in "talking head" format. You should describe your product thoroughly as well as all the details of your launch. This means you should mention your funnel and commission model, your contest and prizes, and so on. Ultimately your video should end by thanking JVs for considering your launch and repeating your invitation.

## Funnel and Commission Model

Your sales funnel diagram would typically be the same place you lay out your commission model. Ideally, you should have a graphical representation of each step in your funnel indicating all of the upsells and downsells along with the commission percentage for each of those steps and the price of each of those products. Include any different pricing options you have for each of those products. You may specify what each step or product is on this diagram or it is also acceptable to simply label them as OTO 1, 2, etc., but expect some JVs to contact you and ask what those OTOs are.

## Contest and Leaderboard

Usually your contest and leaderboard will be together in the same section. You'll want to show images of your contest prizes if they are physical items as well as other details (i.e. if you're offering cash alternatives for people who don't want the physical prizes). If you have minimum sales requirements for each prize, list those clearly. But be warned, a lot of JVs don't like minimum requirements.

As for the leaderboard, you'll want that posted above or below the contest info. You can manually update the leaderboard yourself periodically or you can use an embedding tool that automatically updates it based on the data from JVZoo, W+, etc. It is not necessary to show the number of sales the contestants are making on the leaderboard and most marketers keep this private.

## JV Email Opt-in Form

You'll be wanting to update your JVs every day on how the launch is going and to encourage them to keep promoting. To do this, you'll need their email address. You should have an easily visible opt-in form for JVs to sign up. An added benefit of this is that on later launches you'll have a list of JVs that you can email and notify about your launches.

## DFY Bonuses

In order to make life easier on your JVs, encourage them to promote, and help them get higher conversions, you should provide done-for-you bonuses. These can simply be repurposed PLR/MRR content (check the licenses and make sure you can use them as bonuses) that you place into a zip file and provide a download link on the JV page. For a course on how to make these bonuses look gorgeous and appealing, see our Viking Bonus Creation course.

Once you've got your bonuses, you'll want to go the extra mile and create a bonus template. This simply means creating an html or WP page with those bonuses on them, maybe some images and a few headlines about your product with a CTA stating "grab these bonuses when you buy [your product] through our link". You then place this into a zip file and your JVs can simply upload it to their website and drive traffic to that bonus page. You can either hire someone on Fiverr to create a basic page like this or use an easy web builder like OptimizePress 2.0 to build it yourself and export the page as an OP2 template (but keep in mind not all your JVs have OP2).

## Email Swipes and Graphics

Affiliates are lazy. Yup, it's true. Just like you need to provide DFY bonuses and bonus pages to them, you also need to provide pre-written emails for them to use. You may find this hard to believe, but if you look closely at the promotional emails in your inbox and then look at the JV pages for those products, you'll notice that even famous, high-level marketers often use pre-written swipes from JV pages. Why? Because it takes time to write a good sales email and even more to fill your email marketing schedule with a whole series of them. Providing JVs with email swipes allows them to copy and paste promotional emails and simply tweak them a bit to make them more unique. I'm not saying ALL JVs care about email swipes, but for many of them, this definitely makes your launch more attractive. At a minimum, you should have one email for each day of your launch, but 2 per day is better and having 4 or 5 scarcity-based ones for the last 48 hours of launch is even better.

In this same section, you can also add an assortment of graphics and banners for people to use in their blogs, sites, and even paid ad campaigns. These are probably used less often, but it's still worth having them. If you aren't sure what sizes or dimensions to provide, you can simply go to Google's AdWords advertising site and look at their guidelines for banner ad sizes. This isn't because you're making these for google, but simply because they cover a broad range of shapes and sizes that can be useful anywhere.

## JV Blog

Some will argue that having a blog is no longer necessary since you can do all your updates via social media. Although a blog is certainly "less" necessary than it may previously have been, it's still a good thing to have because people who aren't connected to you on social media but end up on your JV page will see that there are recent updates and exciting developments. Alternatively, you could embed a feed of some sort (e.g. Twitter feed) onto your JV page where you post these updates.

## Sales Page Preview

To give your affiliates an idea of how attractive your offer will be to their audience, you'll want to add a preview of your sales page. This also allows them to read up on the basics of your product so they can understand it better and write more detailed and accurate promotional content about it.

## Affiliate Registration Button

Arguably the most important part. Make sure you have a big, bright, prominent button on your page inviting affiliates to request an affiliate link for your product. This should link to your affiliate registration/details page on whichever affiliate platform or marketplace you're using.

## Layout

A JV recruiting page can take various forms. Some are a single long page with all of these sections stacked top-to-bottom. Some are "microsites" with a main page and a menu bar at the top linking to other pages for things like swipes, bonuses, and contest info. Whatever form you decide to use, ensure the sections can each be easily reached. One idea, if you use one long page, is to have a floating navbar on top that, when an option is clicked, automatically shifts/scrolls the viewer to the appropriate section of the page.

# Chapter 3:
# Where to Find JVs

So now that you have an awesome JV page up and ready, you need to send some JVs to it. Let's talk about where to find them.

## Launch Announcement Sites

Launch announcement sites are an excellent place to let JVs know about your upcoming launch. The two most popular ones are Muncheye and JV Notify. Both of these have a free level where you can list your upcoming launch. However, to get an extra edge, you might opt to pay for added exposure on these sites. Both of them have paid options that will cause your JV recruiting ads to be more prominent and get more views.

## Affiliate Marketplaces

Another good place to advertise your launch is on the affiliate marketplaces themselves. JVZoo, ClickBank, and WarriorPlus all have paid advertising options that will allow you to get your launch in front of potential JVs. The success rate and ROI of these advertisements will vary quite a bit.

## Facebook Groups

You can also announce your launch in one of the many Facebook JV/launch announcement groups. These groups tend to be private, so you'll have to request to join each of them. There are literally a ton of these groups on Facebook. Many of these groups are like notice boards where everyone posts their launch but very few people read about launches, while others are much more interactive and fruitful. Since it only takes a moment to post in each of these, you might as well post even in the lower quality ones, but just be aware that results will vary.

## Coaches

Arguably, the quickest and easiest way to get a high-level JV on your team is to join their coaching program. Many IM coaches offer to promote your product as part of their coaching package. However, you should typically do this well in advance of your launch or even in advance of your product creation. This is because these coaches desire to work with active students and do not want their coaching programs to become "affiliate for hire" programs. Coaching programs tend to be very expensive, but they are often, ironically, less expensive and more effective than the above-mentioned paid ads that people often spend a lot of money on.

## Your Audience

One often-overlooked source of potential JVs is your own audience. If you've already built an email list or a following on social media or your blog, there's a good chance that it may include affiliates who would be interested in promoting your launch.

Now that you have a JV page and know where to find JVs, let's discuss some best practices.

# Chapter 4:

# JV Best Practices

There are a lot of best practices to keep in mind when recruiting JVs. Abiding by these as much as you can will help you get the most out of your JV recruiting efforts.

## Timing

Probably one of the most important aspects of your JV recruitment is timing. If you are hoping to reach out to high-level JVs, you must do it well in advance. High-level affiliates usually have determined what launches they will promote around 4-8 weeks in advance. At a minimum, you must approach these JVs 5 or 6 weeks in advance and have your product ready for them to review.  For lower level affiliates, earlier still tends to better, but it's not as necessary and many low to mid-level affiliates actually decide what they'll promote only a week or so in advance and sometimes even the night before (remember, affiliates tend to be lazy).

## Prizes

Prizes are an important part of your JV incentives. Although, when given a choice, most affiliates will simply opt for a cash prize, it is still a good idea to have physical items on your prize list. These can be generic gadgets and gizmos or prizes that are related to your product's theme. Obviously, a higher cash prize will attract and motivate more than a smaller one, but don't break the bank over prize money. As added incentive, consider having extra contests for things like speed (whoever hits 25 sales fastest) or contests for each day of the launch.

## Commission

If a buyers list is your priority, rather than profit – and it should be – then the indisputable best commission rate is 100%. 100% commission launches automatically pop out and appear more attractive when JVs are looking at upcoming launches. Remember, your launch is not the only one out there, vying for affiliates. If an affiliate can make more money with other launches, he or she will ignore yours. So, if your front-end product is less than $20, you should seriously consider 100% commissions (you can always drop it to 50% after the launch). If your front-end product is higher than $20, then it is acceptable to offer something like 50% or 75%. The most common commission rate for the rest of a funnel is 50%.

## Resources

You should be ready to give your JVs all the resources they need to effectively promote your launch. At a minimum, this should include the swipes, graphics, bonuses, and bonus page templates discussed above. These DFY resources make it easier to promote your launch. Make sure they are all simple to use and attractive to the affiliates' audiences. However, there can be other types of resources as well, including demo videos, free review copies or access, unique coupon codes for each affiliate to give out, pre-written blog content, and so on.

## Updates

Keeping your affiliates updated is absolutely critical. Updates should be sent out almost daily leading up to a launch (via email, social, or whatever your primary channel is). These pre-launch updates can include anything that motivates JVs to promote your launch. Some examples might include an email series on "why this product will sell well", updates about high-profile affiliates joining the launch, updates about conversion-boosting additions such as the completion of a sales video or anything that convinces JVs that your product will convert better. And, ultimately, you need reminder/motivational emails telling your JVs to get ready on the eve of the launch.

During the launch, updates should be going out at least daily across all channels stressing the positive aspects of your product's performance. These are also an excellent opportunity to galvanize your JVs into action with a bit of teasing and provocation about who is beating who on the leader board.

## Reciprocation

Reciprocation belongs both at the beginning of the JV relationship and at the end of any given launch. What that means is that you can offer reciprocation in advance in order to get JVs on board. These "advance" forms of reciprocation can include promises to place a marketer's offer in your post-launch auto-responder, members' area, or bonus page. You can also offer some form of freelancing work (video, copywriting) as reciprocation. The second half of reciprocation comes after your launch in the form of delivering on promises and making an effort to promote their future launches in general.

# Battle Plan

Step 1: Draft up a lucrative plan for your commission model, contest prizes, and other incentives.

Step 2: Set up a thorough JV page with all of the elements mentioned in chapter 2.

Step 3: Use the above-mentioned places to find or advertise to JVs well in advance of your launch.

www.ingramcontent.com/pod-product-compliance
Lightning Source LLC
Chambersburg PA
CBHW071445210326

41597CB00020B/3947